STEM IN SOCCER

SportsZone

An Imprint of Abdo Publishing
abdopublishing.com

BY MEG MARQUARDT

ABDOPUBLISHING.COM

Published by Abdo Publishing, a division of ABDO, PO Box 398166, Minneapolis, Minnesota 55439. Copyright © 2018 by Abdo Consulting Group, Inc. International copyrights reserved in all countries. No part of this book may be reproduced in any form without written permission from the publisher. SportsZone™ is a trademark and logo of Abdo Publishing.

Printed in the United States of America, North Mankato, Minnesota
102017
012018

THIS BOOK CONTAINS
RECYCLED MATERIALS

Cover Photo: Joshua Weisberg/Icon Sportswire/AP Images
Interior Photos: Joshua Weisberg/Icon Sportswire/AP Images, 1; Shutterstock Images, 4–5, 10, 17 (top), 17 (bottom), 34, 43; Jon Super/AP Images, 7; Paul Sancya/AP Images, 8–9; Steve Debenport/ iStockphoto, 12–13; Felice Calabro/AP Images, 15; Kyodo/AP Images, 20–21; Ian Tuttle/BPI/REX/ Shutterstock/AP Images, 22–23; Anna Kutukova/Shutterstock Images, 25; Blazej Lyjak/Shutterstock Images, 27; Le Do/Shutterstock Images, 28–29; Michael Sohn/AP Images, 31 (top); Luca Bruno/AP Images, 31 (middle); David Vincent/AP Images, 31 (bottom); Joe Petro/Icon Sportswire/AP Images, 33; Kevork Djansezian/AP Images, 36–37; Tony Gutierrez/AP Images, 38–39; Mikkel Bigandt/ Shutterstock Images, 40; Stephen Mcsweeny/Shutterstock Images, 44

Editor: Arnold Ringstad
Series Designer: Maggie Villaume
Content Consultant: Misti R. Wajciechowski, M.Ed., Assistant Professor, Teaching and Learning, Virginia Commonwealth University

PUBLISHER'S CATALOGING-IN-PUBLICATION DATA

Names: Marquardt, Meg, author.
Title: STEM in soccer / by Meg Marquardt.
Description: Minneapolis, Minnesota : Abdo Publishing, 2018. | Series: STEM in sports | Includes online resources and index.
Identifiers: LCCN 2017946906 | ISBN 9781532113536 (lib.bdg.) | ISBN 9781532152412 (ebook)
Subjects: LCSH: Soccer--Juvenile literature. | Sports sciences--Juvenile literature. | Physics-- Juvenile literature.
Classification: DDC 796.334--dc23
LC record available at https://lccn.loc.gov/2017946906

TABLE OF CONTENTS

From youth soccer to the professional level, STEM concepts are always in play.

1

KICKING AROUND WITH STEM

The game comes down to this one kick. The goalkeeper is on her toes. As she prepares to defend her goal, her mind swirls with statistics about her opponent. She's trying to remember what she has learned about the player preparing to take the shot. She knows that 8 out of 10 times, this player tries to shoot the ball into the lower right corner of the goal. The keeper knows anything can happen on this kick. But with the math in mind, she prepares to dive.

Out on the field, the star striker lines up her shot. This is the last penalty kick of the game. Right now, the teams are tied. If she scores, her team wins. She knows that she is facing the best goalie in the league. So it's time to pull out a trick shot.

She steps a few feet away from the ball before running at it full speed. With the inside of her foot, she strikes the ball at the perfect angle. The ball lifts into the air. At first, it looks like it's going right down the middle. But a closer look reveals it is spinning. As it spins, the air curves around it. Suddenly, the air starts to force the ball to curve. The goalie, expecting the usual shot to the right, lunges the wrong way. The ball curves left past her and sails into the net.

THE WORLD'S MOST POPULAR SPORT

Soccer, known as football outside the United States, is the most popular sport in the world. An estimated

Soccer is a fast-paced sport with precise kicking and acrobatic goalkeeping.

1 billion people watched the 2014 Men's World Cup final. Worldwide, almost 270 million people play soccer. The sport continues to increase in popularity.

From youth leagues to professional games, soccer players are some of the top athletes in the world. Players pass, kick, and shoot the ball. Defenders chase down

ball carriers and try to steal balls away. Goalkeepers reach and dive to pull off miraculous saves. Soccer is fast-paced action that requires skill and endurance. It is fun for fans and players alike.

Fans often gather to watch big games in public areas, showing strong emotions when their team is doing well or poorly.

STEM IN SOCCER

It might not be easy to see at first, but soccer is full of science, technology, engineering, and math (STEM) principles. Science is at the heart of soccer. Each pass

Each part of the sport, from coaches' preparations to players' training to the game itself, involves many STEM disciplines.

and shot on goal is a feat of physics. Athletes also use the sciences of exercise and nutrition to stay in shape. Science is important to growing a perfectly green soccer field, too.

Technology is also important. Devices tell when a ball has crossed the goal line. Athletes also wear technology to help measure their performance. Body cameras and sensors give them feedback during practice to help them pick out ways to improve.

Engineering is another aspect of STEM that might not seem apparent in soccer right away. But engineers help design the gear that players wear, such as cleats and shin guards. They also create the most important part of the sport: the soccer ball itself.

Math is also important in soccer. Players have to know the angles of each kick to pass to a teammate. They can also learn the precise angle to kick a ball to make it curve a certain way. They need to be aware of the opposing players' habits. Statistics help coaches and teams predict how the competition might pass or shoot.

STEM sets the tone of every soccer game. The best players use science and math to make jaw-dropping shots or saves. Researchers investigate ways to make grass greener and soccer balls more aerodynamic. STEM concepts come together to help make the most popular game on Earth even more exciting.

Whether the ball is rolling along the grass or flying through the air, players need a good grasp of physics to maintain control.

2

SCIENCE ON THE FIELD

Soccer players are experts in physics. They might not be able to carry out complex equations on a blackboard. But they do know about the forces and motion that go into kicking a soccer ball. With practice, soccer players learn how to harness physics. Along with players, field managers and referees also use science to help them make the game exciting, fair, and safe.

KICKING AROUND WITH PHYSICS

Soccer science is controlled by Newtonian mechanics. This branch of physics is named for the English scientist Sir Isaac Newton. Newton worked in the 1600s and 1700s. He created a field of study that describes the way objects move and interact with each other. For example, when a soccer player kicks a ball, the ball's motion follows laws that Newton discovered.

In his work, Newton described three laws of motion. One of these laws states that an object that is sitting still needs something to put it into motion. This means that a soccer ball isn't going to go anywhere unless someone kicks it. But once it does get going, it takes some other force to stop it. This could come from another player's foot. It could also be friction from the grass.

Newton's laws also help describe what happens when the ball is in motion. When a player kicks the ball, he transfers energy to it. How fast the ball goes depends on how hard the player strikes the ball. Newton's physics

Professional players kick the ball with incredible force.

uses a simple equation to describe how this works. Force is equal to mass multiplied by acceleration. Players use their muscles to accelerate the mass of their foot into the ball. That force sends the ball flying.

A good soccer player learns how to utilize Newton's laws with finesse. He knows how fast the grass will slow down a rolling ball and just how hard to kick the ball to pass it to a teammate.

GROWING GREENER GRASS

Creating a green field is a feat of agricultural science. Soccer fields are often made of a tough type of grass, such as ryegrass. This grass can stand up to the wear and tear of games and practices. However, even the toughest grass will start to turn brown and die off after repeated use. The field manager's real challenge is keeping the turf a bright green.

One tool in a field manager's arsenal is aeration. When players or mowing equipment go over the field, they pack the soil down. That makes it hard for moisture and air to get to the grass's root system. Field managers use special aeration tools to pull out small pieces of soil. When these soil cores are removed, air and water can get back into the soil, helping grass bounce back to life. Science helps prepare the field for game day.

AERATING MACHINE

AIR   WATER

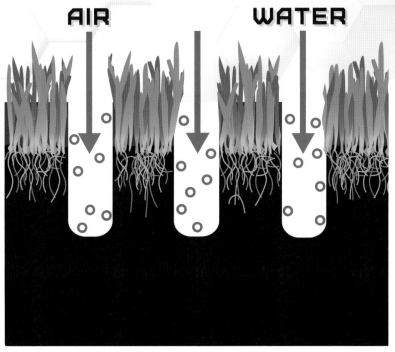

Aeration works because it helps roots grow more deeply. It leaves wide open holes in the soil. These holes allow water and air to get into the soil. The process also promotes new growth. As the soil slowly fills back in, grass roots can grow longer and stronger. This makes for healthier, hardier grass for soccer fields.

AERATION

VANISHING SPRAY

If a player on one team commits a foul, the other team gets a free kick. A free kick is just what it sounds like. The kicker gets to pass or shoot the ball without any interference. The opposing team needs to stay at least 10 yards (9 m) away from the kicker.

Referees estimate how far away the defenders need to stand. But until recent years, defenders often crept forward to gain an advantage. Thanks to the science of chemistry, that's no longer possible. To help referees

SCIENCE IN ACTION

GOING GREEN

Millions of people travel to the World Cup. All that travel means a lot of pollution from planes, trains, and cars. In 2008, the organizers of the World Cup took steps to counteract some of those emissions. They picked projects that would help communities. For example, one project in South Africa converted the way citrus farms power their operations. Instead of using coal, some now use sawdust, which emits less pollution. By taking this step, FIFA and the World Cup helped make the impact of the game more environmentally friendly.

keep control of the game, they use special vanishing spray. It is made up of chemicals such as butane and propane. These chemicals mix with a foaming agent. When the referee presses down on the nozzle, a white foam is laid down on the field. Defenders have to stay behind the line or risk being called for a foul. In a few minutes, the foam evaporates.

ATHLETE NUTRITION

Nutrition, or the science of food, is important in soccer, too. Players are running almost nonstop during the game, so they have to have the right kind of fuel to keep going. Carbohydrates provide this fuel. Protein repairs muscle tissue. Soccer players focus on eating lean meats and as many fruits and vegetables as possible. Since they work out hard during practices and games, players often have a post-workout snack of some kind. This helps them regain the energy they just burned off with healthy refueling.

One type of ball with a built-in sensor is connected wirelessly to a watch worn by referees.

CHAPTER

3

THE GOALS OF TECHNOLOGY

Soccer seems like it might be a game that doesn't rely much on technology. After all, it can be played with just players and a ball. But technology can have a big impact on the sport. One of the most commonly used pieces of technology is the goal line sensor. Other types of sensors, both inside the ball and on players' clothes, help bring technology to the game too.

GOAL LINE SENSORS

The most important moments in any soccer game are shots on goal. In order for a goal to count, the ball has to cross the white line between the goal posts. This white line is called a goal line. However, in the moment, it's not always easy for a referee to see exactly where the ball

GOAL

was when the keeper stopped it. Even though
referees are highly trained, sometimes they
make mistakes that can cost a team the game.

To cut down on human error, some soccer leagues
have started to use goal line sensors. This technology
can map exactly where a ball goes on the field.

Some setups use cameras all over the field, not just on the goalposts. This allows the system to calculate a shot's complete path from when it leaves the kicker's foot to when it lands in the goal.

This sort of technology can let the referee know instantly if a goal has been scored. Some referees wear a watch that is hooked up to the tracking system. When the ball crosses the goal line, his watch lights up with capital letters: GOAL.

SENSORS IN A BALL

Another version of goal line technology uses a magnetic field. The goal posts are covered in wires. Between them, a magnetic field is generated. Inside the soccer ball, there are more lightweight wires.

The wires in the ball are key. When the ball crosses the goal line, it disrupts the magnetic field. A player or referee crossing the line can't cause the same disruption. When referees review the data, they can be confident that if the field is disrupted, it's only because of the ball.

1. Equipment in the frame of the goal creates a magnetic field.

3. Sensors study the changes in the magnetic field to determine the ball's exact position.

2. The ball has copper coils inside. When it approaches the goal's magnetic field, the magnetic field changes slightly.

One type of goal line technology uses a magnetic field. The magnetic field is analyzed by a large antenna off the field. When a ball approaches the magnetic field, the antenna senses that. That antenna can then send a message to the referee that a goal has been scored.

This sort of technology makes certain a goal is counted. Or, just as important, it can make sure that a ball that didn't actually make it into the goal isn't counted.

WEARABLE TECH

Technology isn't only about scoring goals. It's about setting goals, too. Players often use wearable tech to help track their performance. Some of the tech is simple. It might monitor how fast and far a player is running. It could report on heart rate. Wearable tech can also get

ROBOTS PLAYING SOCCER

Sports are a great way to test the limits of robotics. Athletics require a lot of coordination, but they also require a lot of smarts. Roboticists have to make robots that can move around the field. The robots also have to know when to pass and how to set up goal shots. Each year there is a World Cup, there is also a RoboCup. At the RoboCup, different teams of roboticists pit their creations against each other. This sort of competition drives new innovations in robots. With each new RoboCup, the robots become smarter, more capable players. Still, it will probably be a long time before they are as good as the human players in the real World Cup.

Fitness watches have become popular with all kinds of athletes.

more specific. Some devices measure a player's posture as they run. This can help them make corrections to improve their speed.

Cleats help players stay agile on slippery grass, and shin guards protect their legs.

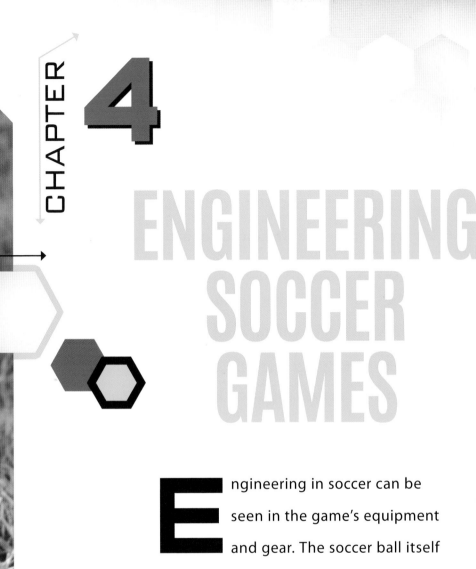

4

ENGINEERING SOCCER GAMES

Engineering in soccer can be seen in the game's equipment and gear. The soccer ball itself undergoes careful engineering to make sure an expert player can handle the ball well. Cleats and shin guards are carefully designed to help players be quick and mobile while also staying safe.

DESIGNING THE BALL

From far away, a soccer ball may look like a perfectly round ball. Up close, it's a different story. Soccer balls are full of seams. The most iconic ball is the black and white one. These balls are made of 32 different panels. The panels are pentagons and hexagons. However, other balls have different numbers of panels. There may be anywhere from 6 to 32 of them. These panels come in different shapes and sizes. Because the shapes of the panels change, there are subtle changes in how the ball moves through the air.

For example, the 2014 World Cup ball had only six panels. This ball is known as the Brazuca. Fewer panels means fewer seams and fewer places where stitching is apparent. When air catches on the stitching, the airflow is disrupted. This can make the ball's path more unpredictable. With relatively few panels, the 2014 World Cup ball moved smoothly through the air.

2006 WORLD CUP, GERMANY

2010 WORLD CUP, SOUTH AFRICA

2014 WORLD CUP, BRAZIL

Soccer ball surfaces are an impressive use of geometry. The panels have to fit together perfectly to make a ball-like shape. Sometimes the panels are rigid geometric shapes, such as pentagons or hexagons. But some balls, such as the one used in the 2014 World Cup, are made up of more flowing shapes. For each World Cup, engineers design a new ball. The small changes may make the balls move differently when rolling or flying through the air.

For a professional player playing in the world's biggest tournament, such engineering makes a big difference.

GEAR

Soccer players compete in special shoes called cleats. Cleats have a series of spikes or studs on the bottom. This lets the shoes dig into the grass and avoid slipping. Cleats allow players to change direction quickly without losing their footing.

A KNUCKLE BALL

The 2010 World Cup ball was called the Jabulani. During the competition, players complained about how it handled. When kicked at top speeds, it seemed to veer off course. When that happens, it's called knuckling. The ball took erratic, unexpected turns. The effect can be seen in some baseball pitches, too. In baseball, the pitcher wants the knuckling to happen. In soccer, knuckling is a negative effect. The Jabulani upset players so much that they began calling it a "supermarket ball." This insult was harsh to engineers who had spent so much time making what they thought was the perfect ball. But sometimes even the best in the business can make a ball that turns out not to work as expected.

Cleats have different shapes based on the type of grass being played on.

Cleats are not just an afterthought in soccer gearing. They take center stage. For the 2016 Olympics, engineers spent a lot of time thinking about the top of the shoe. They wanted to make a shoe that was better at gripping

Players can choose gear that works for their game and matches their personal style.

the ball. If the shoe has a flat, slippery surface, the ball can slide off. Engineers created a shoe with grooves and peaks. It is made out of 3D-printed yarn. When the ball hits those shoes, the material absorbs some of the impact rather than letting the ball just bounce off. That way the player can have more control over the ball.

Shin guards, or shin pads, are an important part of soccer safety. A shin guard covers the front of the leg from ankle to knee. It is typically made of durable plastic. Since kicking is the main thing that happens in a soccer game, shins can take a real beating. Shin guards protect against bruising, cuts, or even broken bones.

Shin guards aren't one-size-fits-all. Different players use different guards designed for their position. For instance, a goalkeeper, who isn't in the middle of the action, needs only lightweight ones. A defender may need much heavier protection.

Retired soccer star David Beckham was well known for his ability to bend the ball around defenders to score goals.

5

BEND IT WITH MATH

Math is everywhere in soccer. Players need to know how to shoot the ball at the best angles. They also need to know how to time passes and shots. And the very best players learn the best mathematical trick of all. They learn how to bend a kick, making it take an unexpected angle through the air.

THE PERFECT PASS

It might seem like the shot on goal is the only kick that matters in soccer. But in reality, all the kicks that come before a shot are just as important. The passes that set up a shot have to be precise. The ball has to reach teammates who are in the middle of defenders. All of this requires players to know a lot about math.

One thing players learn about is relative speed, or how fast they are going compared to the person they are passing to. The goal is to get off a lead pass. A lead pass reaches a player while she is still mid-run. That way the player doesn't have to slow down at all. The player can just take the ball and keep pushing toward the goal. But to pull this off, the passer needs to time the kick perfectly. She must kick the ball to where her teammate is going to be, rather than where the teammate is right now.

Players often have to track down a pass in mid-run to stay ahead of the other team.

Shooting from the front of the goal gives players the most angles to choose from.

ANGLES ON GOAL

A soccer goal might look like a big target, but in reality it can be tricky to get a shot in. It's easy for a player to kick the ball too high or too wide. In order to score a goal, players have to practice kicking perfect angles.

If a soccer player were standing directly in front of the middle of the goal, he or she would have a pretty big opening to hit. But the farther to the side a player goes, the smaller the opening becomes. Imagine trying to throw a crumpled piece of paper through an open door. Right in front of the door, this is easy. But standing right against the wall, it's almost impossible to get the paper through.

Soccer players face the same challenge. A player standing all the way to the right side of the goal can only take a shot on the far left side. They are standing at too sharp of an angle to make the ball go in. Unless, of course, they can get the ball to bend.

MAGNUS EFFECT

Good soccer players can do more than kick in a straight line. They also learn how to put some curve into the ball's path. This type of curving is called the Magnus effect. It all comes down to the way the ball leaves the player's foot. If a player hits the ball with the inside of her foot, she can send it off with a bit of spin.

That spin causes a change in airflow. As the ball spins, it causes the air around it to move. The air moves around the ball in the same direction the ball is spinning. This causes the ball to be pushed slightly off course from straight. The ball's path bends in midair. Even if a player is standing at a really wide angle, they can take advantage of the Magnus effect to hook the ball into the goal.

The mathematical part of the Magnus effect still comes down to angles. How fast the ball spins depends

SOCCER AND MATH EDUCATION

Romania, a country in Europe, struggles with a high rate of school dropouts. In 2016, its men's soccer team tried a new way to help get kids excited about math. In a training session for a match against Spain, its players wore jerseys with math problems on the back. Solving the problems would give the players' actual numbers. For instance, one player's jersey said, "(6×5-4)/2." His number was 13. A Romanian soccer official said, "We want to have a healthy generation and smart students who achieve performance and tools through tailored passions. Through this project, children will learn the basics of football and have an opportunity for the first time in our country— to discover mathematics through an attractive approach."

RESULTING FLIGHT PATH

DIRECTION OF FORCE FROM KICK

SPIN

DIRECTION OF FORCE FROM MAGNUS EFFECT

DIRECTION OF FORCE FROM KICK

+ DIRECTION OF FORCE FROM MAGNUS EFFECT (CAUSED BY SPIN)

RESULTING FLIGHT PATH

The force of a kick launches a soccer ball into the air in a specific direction. However, when the ball is spinning, the Magnus effect adds another influence to the ball's motion. This results in a curved flight path that confuses defenders and makes amazing goals possible.

Goalies must anticipate the angle of a shot to make a thrilling
diving save.

on the angle that the ball is struck at. How much a

player wants the ball to spin depends on where she is

standing in relation to the goal. A perfect Magnus effect

shot takes a lot of practice before a player knows how to intuitively handle all those angles. But once she does, she can kick one of the hardest-to-stop goals.

SOCCER: A CHAMPION OF STEM

From growing a greener field to calculating the perfect pass, STEM fields help make the sport work and give soccer players a chance to work to their full potential. Technology helps keep the game fair with goal line sensors. And engineering keeps players safe and geared in the best equipment.

The ball itself is perhaps the best example of STEM. Science dictates how it moves through the air. It can be fitted with technology for goal line sensors. Its structure and surface are carefully engineered. And a player must consider the mathematics of angles when taking a tricky shot. STEM is at the heart of the world's most popular game.

GLOSSARY

AERATION
To circulate air through soil.

FORCE
Energy acting on an object.

FRICTION
The force that results when two objects rub against each other.

GEOMETRY
The branch of math dealing with shapes.

MAGNETIC FIELD
An area in which a nearby magnet's influence can be detected.

MECHANICS
A branch of science dealing with force and motion.

ROBOTICIST
Someone who designs and builds robots.

SEAM
A place where pieces of a soccer ball's surface are stitched together.

TURF
The playing field.

ONLINE RESOURCES

To learn more about STEM in soccer, visit **abdobooklinks.com**. These links are routinely monitored and updated to provide the most current information available.

MORE INFORMATION

BOOKS

Kortemeier, Todd. *Total Soccer*. Minneapolis, MN: Abdo Publishing, 2017.

Marthaler, Jon. *Soccer Trivia*. Minneapolis, MN: Abdo Publishing, 2016.

Monnig, Alex. *The World Cup*. Minneapolis, MN: Abdo Publishing, 2013.

INDEX

ABOUT THE AUTHOR

Meg Marquardt started as a scientist but decided she liked writing about science even more. She enjoys researching physics, geology, and climate science. She lives in Madison, Wisconsin, with her two scientist cats, Lagrange and Doppler.